This Computer Science Activity Book belongs to

_____

Daily Words of Affirmation:

I am Smart.

I am Confident.

I am Creative.

I am loved.

I can achieve my dreams.

Fourth edition. ISBN-13: 978-1-7322734-4-3

For information on distribution, translations, or bulk sales, contact:
Innovant Technologies, LLC | C/O Bukola Somide | P.O. Box 44301, Phoenix AZ 85064
info@innovant-tech.com; www.innovant-tech.com

Color & Design Challenge

Name: Somi

Pronounced: [shaw.me]

Age: 8

Hobbies: Dancing, singing, and learning to code

Find My Match <A/>

Find the matching definition for the Computer Science term.
Trace the lines and write the correct answer. Learning is fun!

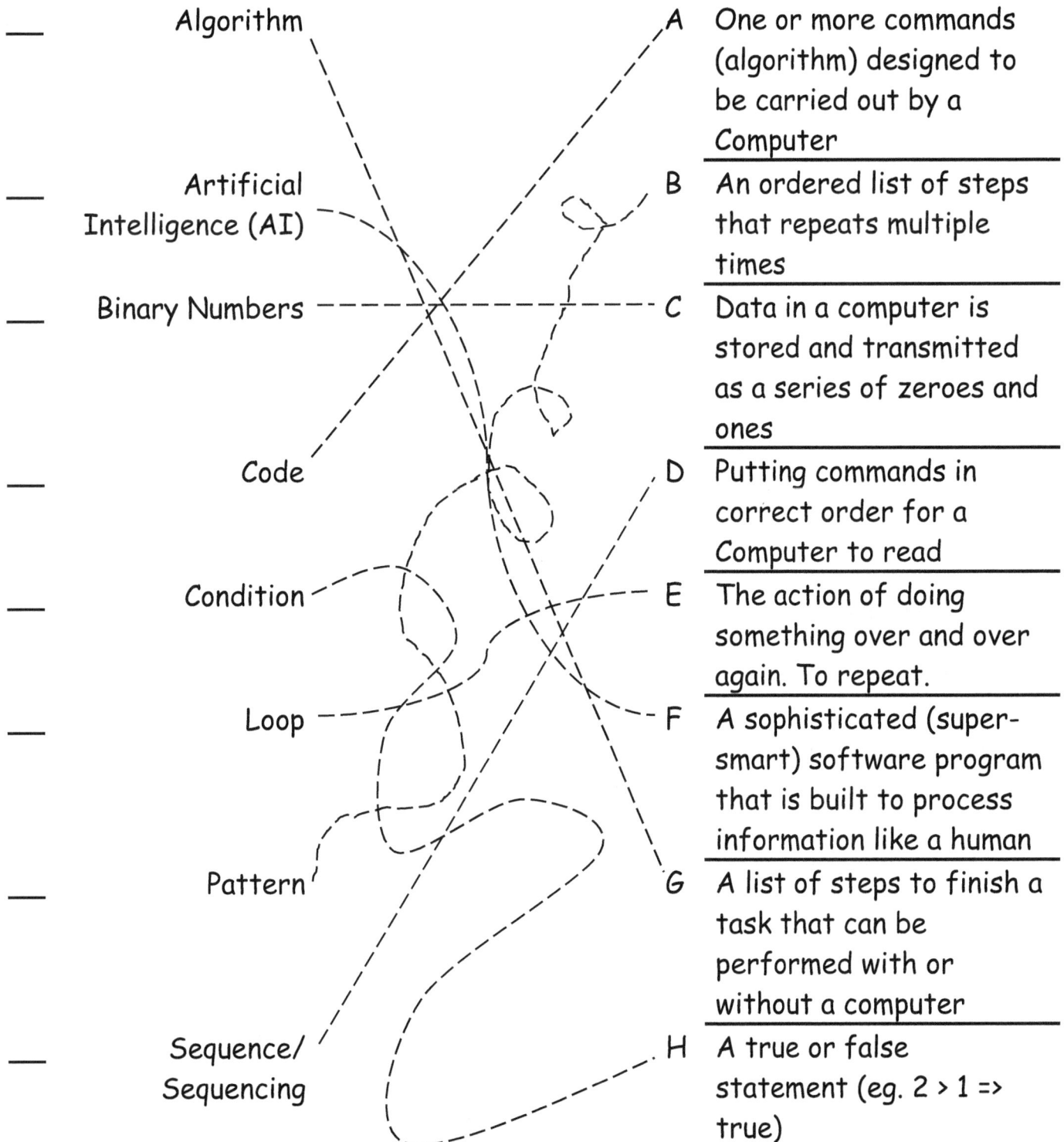

__	Algorithm	**A** One or more commands (algorithm) designed to be carried out by a Computer
__	Artificial Intelligence (AI)	**B** An ordered list of steps that repeats multiple times
__	Binary Numbers	**C** Data in a computer is stored and transmitted as a series of zeroes and ones
__	Code	**D** Putting commands in correct order for a Computer to read
__	Condition	**E** The action of doing something over and over again. To repeat.
__	Loop	**F** A sophisticated (super-smart) software program that is built to process information like a human
__	Pattern	**G** A list of steps to finish a task that can be performed with or without a computer
__	Sequence/ Sequencing	**H** A true or false statement (eg. $2 > 1 \Rightarrow$ true)

Color & Design Challenge

Name: Esmeralda

Nickname: "Esie"

Age: 8

Hobbies: Drawing, fashion design, and learning about cyber security

4

Find My Match <B/>

Find the matching definition for the Computer Science term.
Trace the lines and write the correct answer. Learning is fun!

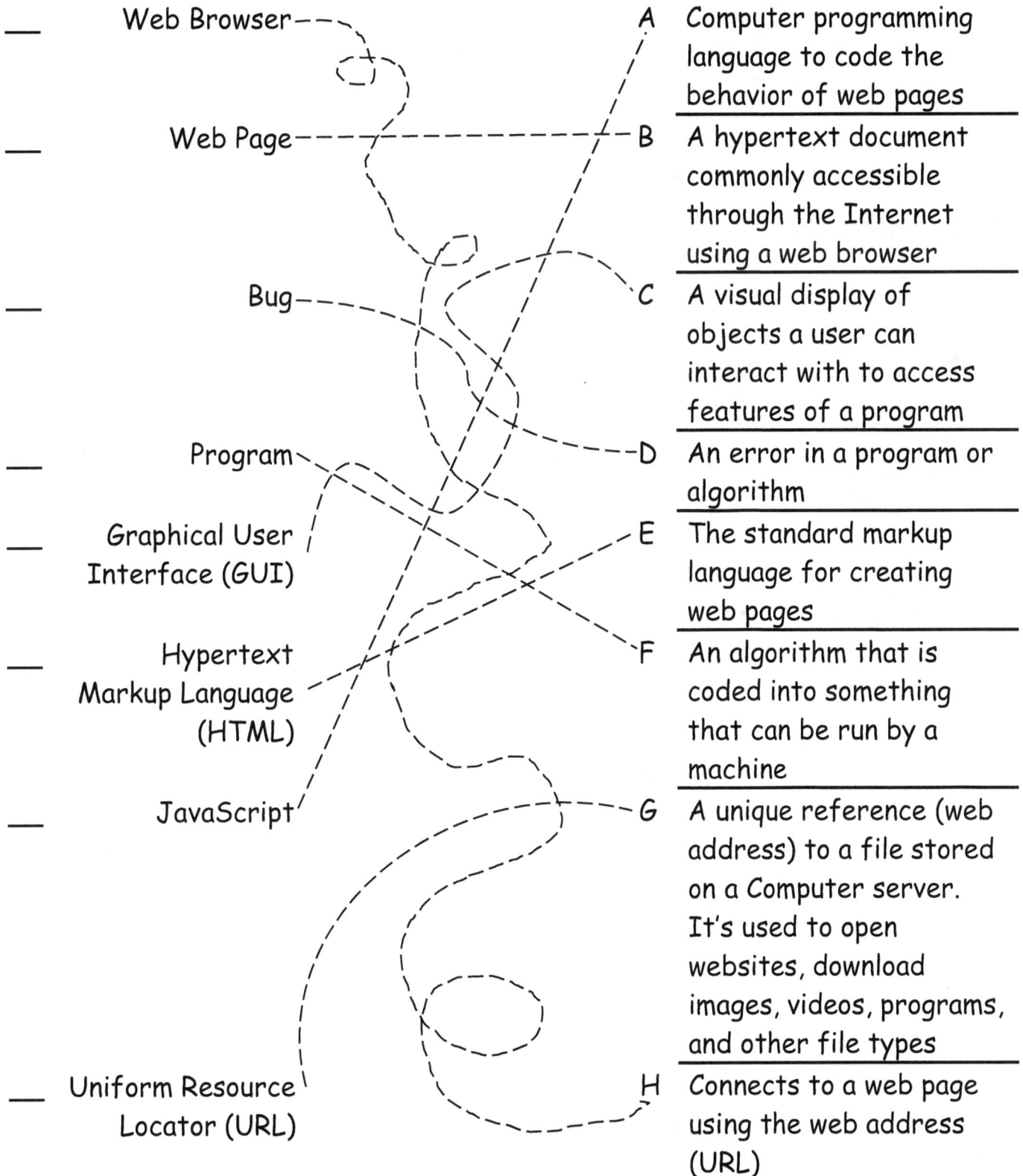

___ Web Browser

___ Web Page

___ Bug

___ Program

___ Graphical User Interface (GUI)

___ Hypertext Markup Language (HTML)

___ JavaScript

___ Uniform Resource Locator (URL)

A Computer programming language to code the behavior of web pages

B A hypertext document commonly accessible through the Internet using a web browser

C A visual display of objects a user can interact with to access features of a program

D An error in a program or algorithm

E The standard markup language for creating web pages

F An algorithm that is coded into something that can be run by a machine

G A unique reference (web address) to a file stored on a Computer server. It's used to open websites, download images, videos, programs, and other file types

H Connects to a web page using the web address (URL)

Spot the Pattern

Pattern: Square, Triangle, Triangle

Pattern repeats two times: Square, Triangle, Triangle

Find and circle the single repeating pattern	How many times does the pattern repeat?
○ ○ ○ △ ○ ○ △	A.
◇ ■ ◇ ■ ◇ ■	B.
□ ▲ △ ▲ △ ▲ △	C.
○ ● ◇ ■ ○ ● ◇ ■ ○ ● ◇ ■ △	D.

Create your own pattern and repeat it two or more times

Sequence This! <A/>

Oops! There are bugs in the algorithm below. The steps with an 'X' are in the wrong order. Swap these buggy steps to fix the instructions. Write the correct order in the third column.

How to fold a hat

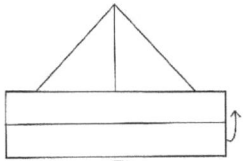
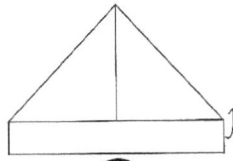
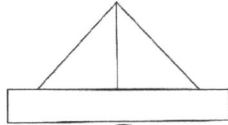
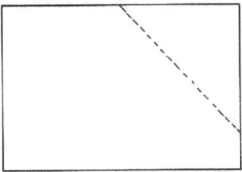
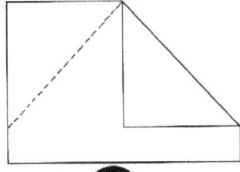
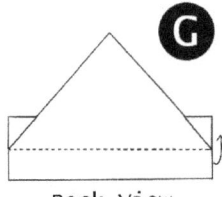

Back View

BUG	STEPS	FIX
X	D	
	E	
X	A	
	C	
	B	
	G	
X	F	

How to fold a boat

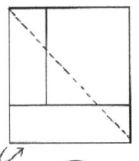
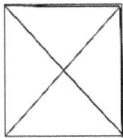
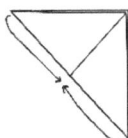
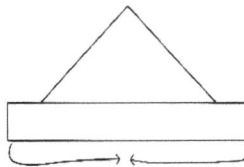

Back View

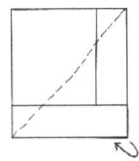
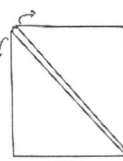

Back View

BUG	STEPS	FIX
	N	
	H	
	J	
	I	
X	M	
X	L	
X	K	

Crossword Puzzle <A/>

Use the clues on the next page to fill out the puzzle below. Have fun Code-Stars!

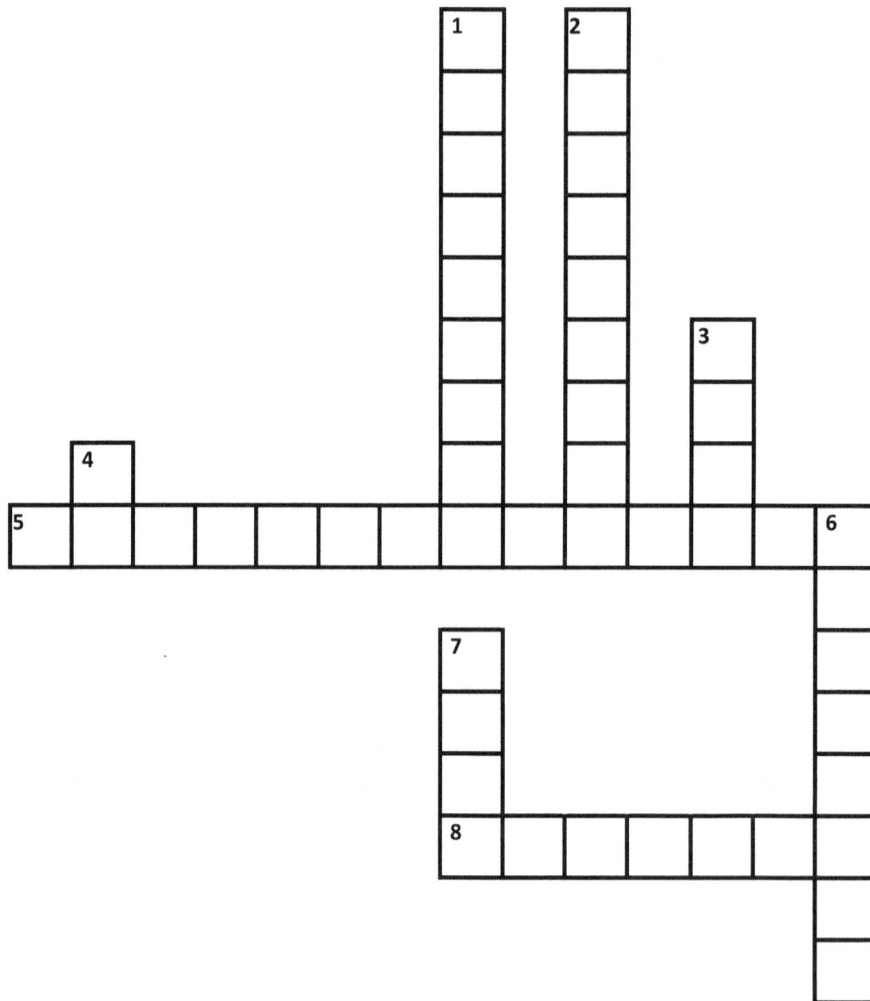

Find the correct word for the short definitions below. Write the answer in its matching number block on the previous page.

QUICK TIP: Review/complete the exercise,

"Find My Match <A/>"

ACROSS

5. Ones and Zeros (e.g. 010101)
8. A sequence of repeating steps

DOWN

1. A true/false statement
2. A list of steps to complete a task
3. A Computer command
4. Two-letter abbreviation for a super-smart program
6. Computer commands in correct order
7. To repeat

Color & Design Challenge

Name: "Princess Somi"

Event: Dressed for her 8th birthday party

Favorite food: Cake

Birthday gift: A cool tablet

Sequence This! <B/>

Order the missing lines of code from the "Code Bin™" into the correct sequence in the "Code Zone™" to match this conditional statement:

If the traffic light is red then stop moving.

Code Bin

```
} //comment: Then close action
```

```
{ //comment: Then begin action
```

```
var traffic_light = "red";
```

```
if( traffic_light == "red" )
```

```
Print( "STOP Moving." );
```

Code Zone

1. var traffic_light = "red"; _____

2. _____

3. { //comment: Then begin action _____

4. _____

5. _____

Crossword Puzzle <B/>

Use the clues on the next page to fill out the puzzle below. Have fun Code-Stars!

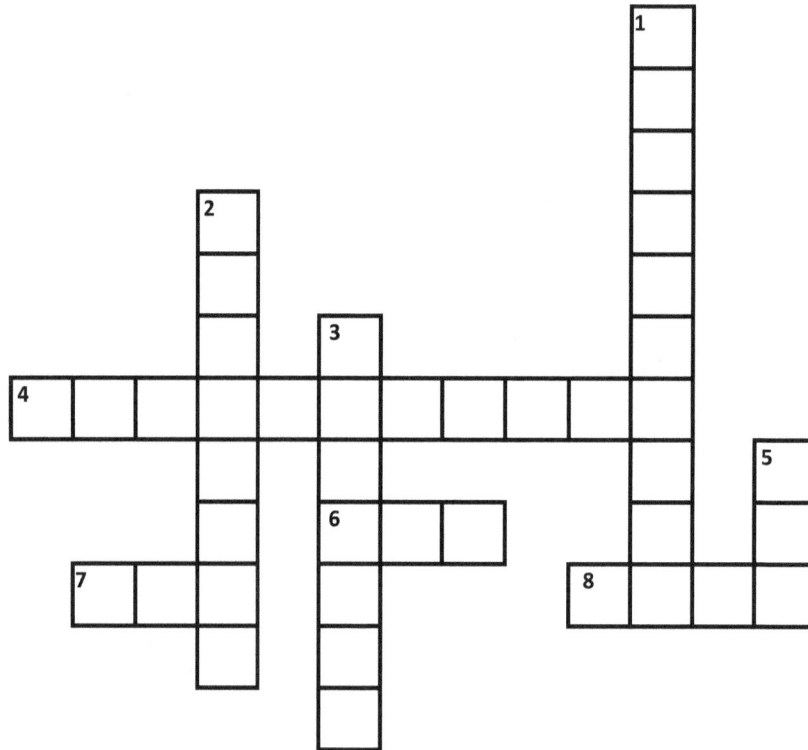

Find the correct word for the short definitions below. Write the answer in its matching number block on the previous page.

QUICK TIP: Review/complete the exercise,

"Find My Match <B/>"

ACROSS

4. Connects to a web page
6. Three-letter abbreviation for a visual display of a Computer program
7. An error in a program or algorithm
8. Four-letter abbreviation for a markup language used to create web pages

DOWN

1. A Computer language
2. Hypertext document accessed through the Internet
3. Code that can be run by a machine
5. Three-letter abbreviation often representing a web address

Alphabet to Binary Numbers Chart

Letter	8-bits Binary Code	Letter	8-bits Binary Code	Letter	8-bits Binary Code	Letter	8-bits Binary Code
A	0100 0001	N	0100 1110	a	0110 0001	n	0110 1110
B	0100 0010	O	0100 1111	b	0110 0010	o	0110 1111
C	0100 0011	P	0101 0000	c	0110 0011	p	0111 0000
D	0100 0100	Q	0101 0001	d	0110 0100	q	0111 0001
E	0100 0101	R	0101 0010	e	0110 0101	r	0111 0010
F	0100 0110	S	0101 0011	f	0110 0110	s	0111 0011
G	0100 0111	T	0101 0100	g	0110 0111	t	0111 0100
H	0100 1000	U	0101 0101	h	0110 1000	u	0111 0101
I	0100 1001	V	0101 0110	i	0110 1001	v	0111 0110
J	0100 1010	W	0101 0111	j	0110 1010	w	0111 0111
K	0100 1011	X	0101 1000	k	0110 1011	x	0111 1000
L	0100 1100	Y	0101 1001	l	0110 1100	y	0111 1001
M	0100 1101	Z	0101 1010	m	0110 1101	z	0111 1010

Write your initials (first letter in your first and last name) in the boxes below, then find and write the correct 8-bits binary code. Use UPPERCASE letters only.

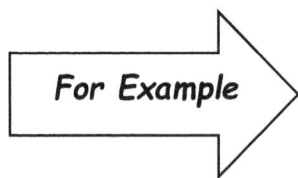

For Example

B	S
0100 0010	0101 0011

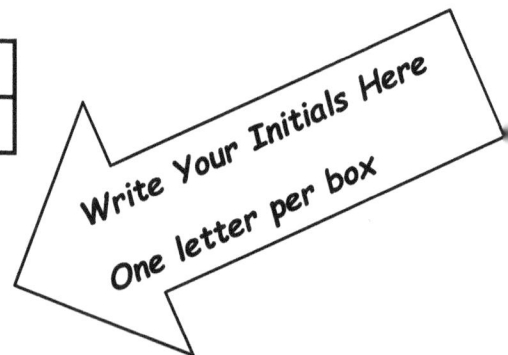

Write Your Initials Here
One letter per box

Decode this! Binary Numbers to Decimal

Finish decoding the decimal value from its binary value equivalent.

Zero (0) means the bit is off and one (1) means the bit is on.

You got this, Code-Star!

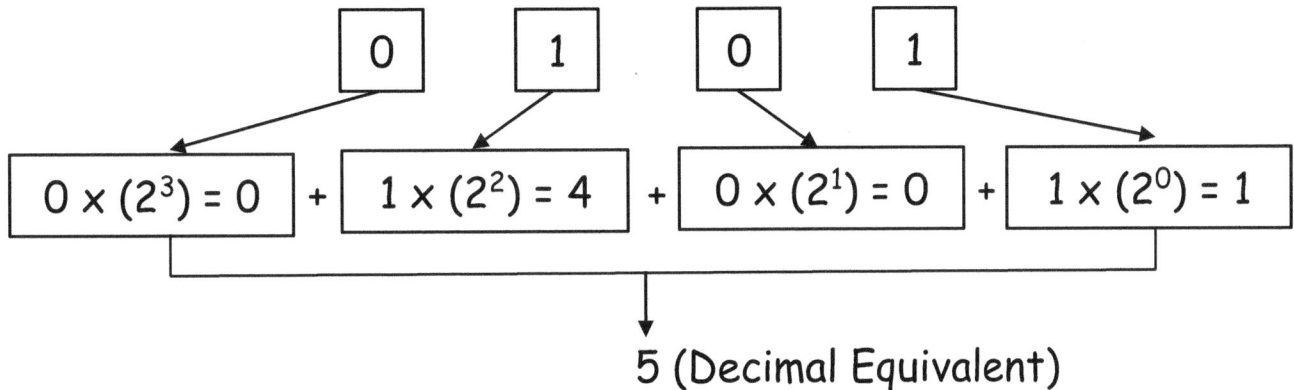

0	1	0	1

$$0 \times (2^3) = 0 \quad + \quad 1 \times (2^2) = 4 \quad + \quad 0 \times (2^1) = 0 \quad + \quad 1 \times (2^0) = 1$$

5 (Decimal Equivalent)

Binary Value	Decoding Formula Calculate the missing values below				Calculate the missing Decimal Values below
	2^3	2^2	2^1	2^0	
	8	4	2	1	
0 0 0 0	0 +	0 +	0 +	0	0
0 0 0 1	0 +	0 +	0 +	1	1
0 0 1 0	0 +	0 +	2 +	0	2
0 0 1 1	0 +	0 +	2 +	1	3
0 1 0 0	0 +	4 +	0 +	0	4
0 1 0 1	0 +	4 +	0 +	1	5
0 1 1 0	0 +	4 +	2 +	0	
0 1 1 1	0 +	4 +	2 +		
1 0 0 0	8 +	0 +		+	
1 0 0 1	8 +	+		+	
1 0 1 0		+	+	+	

\<code\> Game Time! \</code\>

Code-Star, your mission is to collect all the stars in the maze with as little steps as possible. Write step-by-step instructions/commands on the next page.

Have fun!!

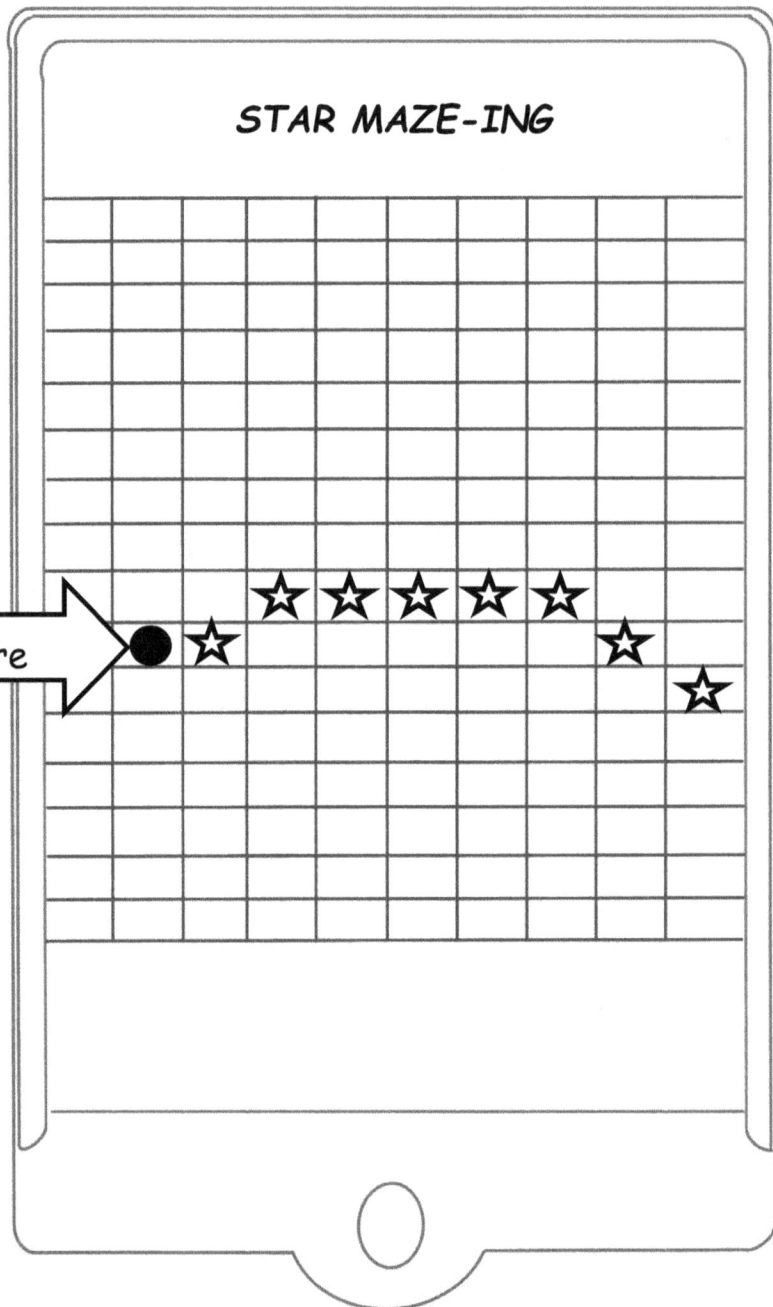

Algorithm Worksheet

Write commands/instructions for "NEXON™", our Artificial Intelligence (AI) program, to process/run.

NOTE: Use the list of commands listed below to navigate the "Star Maze-ing" game. The command to collect a star is included in each instruction.

1. moveForwardOneStep();

2. _____

3. _____

4. _____

5. _____

6. _____

7. _____

8. _____

9. _____

10. _____

11. _____

12. _____

13. _____

moveUpOneStep();

moveDownOneStep();

moveForwardOneStep();

moveBackwardOneStep();

BONUS ACTIVITY: Identify a repeating pattern in your code. Using the Loop bin, write the single code pattern that needs to be repeated. Enter the number of repeats at the top (_).

Loop(__)

_____

_____

_____

_____

Gaming Grid Pad

Create your own gaming rules, objects, and mission. Add obstacles (wall, hole, bug, aliens etc). Think outside-the-box, Code-Star.

Algorithm Worksheet

Write commands/instructions for "NEXON™", our Artificial Intelligence (AI) program, to process/run.

1. _____

2. _____

3. _____

4. _____

5. _____

6. _____

7. _____

8. _____

9. _____

10. _____

11. _____

12. _____

13. _____

For example, jumpOver();

Map The Keywords

Fill in the bubbles with the correct keyword. Choose from the list below.

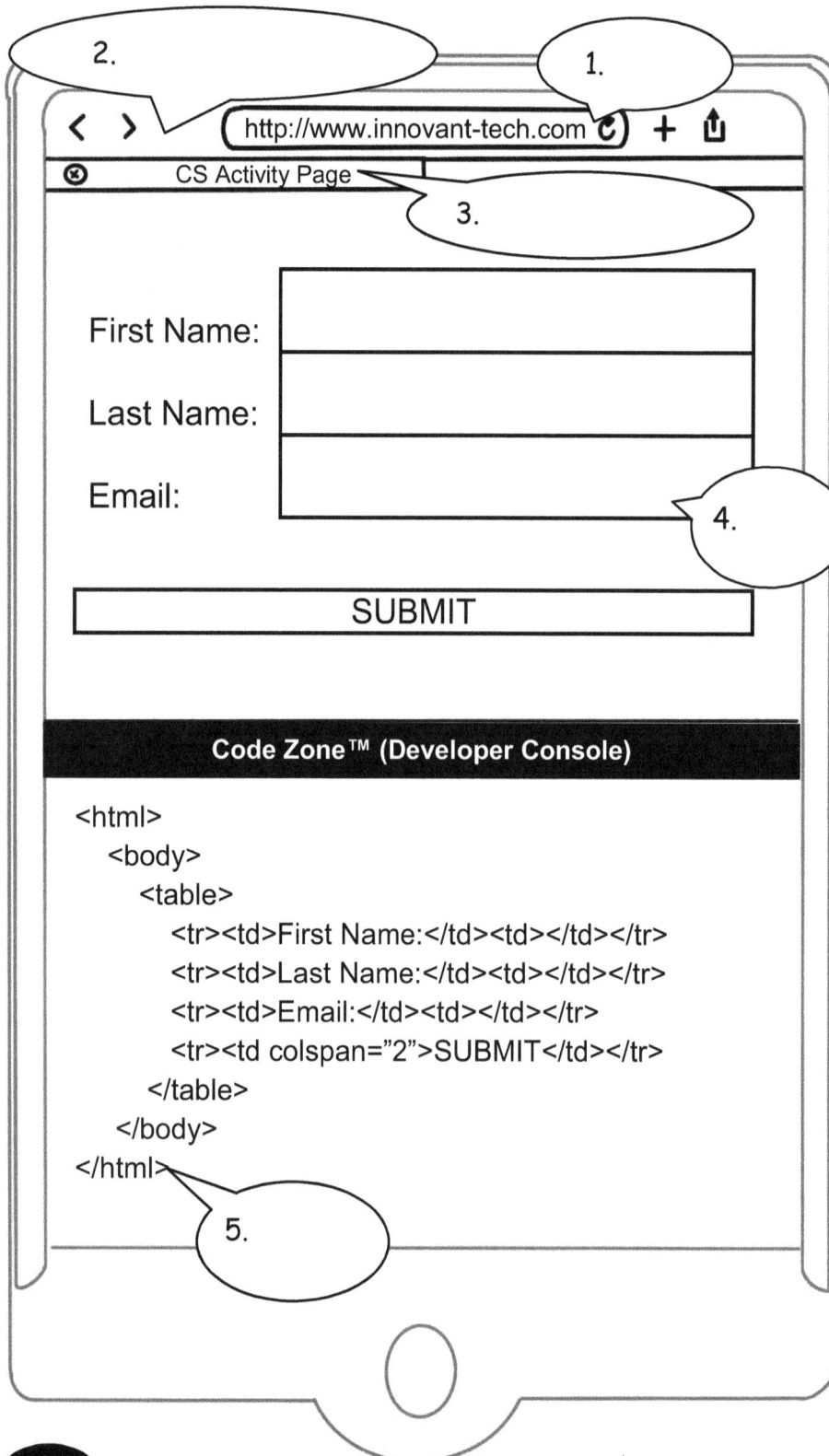

2.

1.

http://www.innovant-tech.com ⟳ + ⬆

⊗ CS Activity Page

3.

First Name:

Last Name:

Email:

4.

SUBMIT

Keywords:

o HTML
o Web Page
o URL or
  Web Address
o Web Browser
o GUI

Code Zone™ (Developer Console)

```
<html>
  <body>
    <table>
      <tr><td>First Name:</td><td></td></tr>
      <tr><td>Last Name:</td><td></td></tr>
      <tr><td>Email:</td><td></td></tr>
      <tr><td colspan="2">SUBMIT</td></tr>
    </table>
  </body>
</html>
```

5.

NOTE: The code shown here is just for illustration purposes.

20

Secret Mission!

Hi there,

Congratulations, Code-Star! You made it through this activity book. Hope you found the activities entertaining and educational.

I'm the author of "Somi The Computer Scientist" children's storybook series. I have a secret mission for you to accomplish.

Are you ready?

MISSION ACCEPTED:

Simply **crack the code below**, find the missing letters using the binary number clues to complete the URL. Once done, go to the web address to **unlock the mystery activity/gift**. But hurry, time is running out. The web address could expire at any time.

Happy Decoding!!

___	___	___	___	___
0110 0010	0110 1111	0110 1110	0111 0101	0111 0011

___	___	___	___
0110 0111	0110 0001	0110 1101	0110 0101

https://www.innovant-tech.com/ _ _ _ _ _ _ _ _ _

Answer Key

Find My Match <A/>	**Find My Match <B/>**
✓ G, F, C, A, H, E, B, D	✓ H, B, D, F, C, E, A, G

Spot The Pattern

    A. 2 (circle, circle, triangle)

    B. 3 (diamond, shaded-square)

    C. 3 (shaded-triangle, triangle, shaded-triangle, triangle)

    D. 3 (circle, shaded-circle, diamond, shaded-square)

Sequence This! <A/>

  ✓ Hat Steps - Bug Fix: A, E, F, C, B, G, D

  ✓ Boat Steps - Bug Fix: N, H, J, I, L, K, M

Crossword Puzzle <A/>

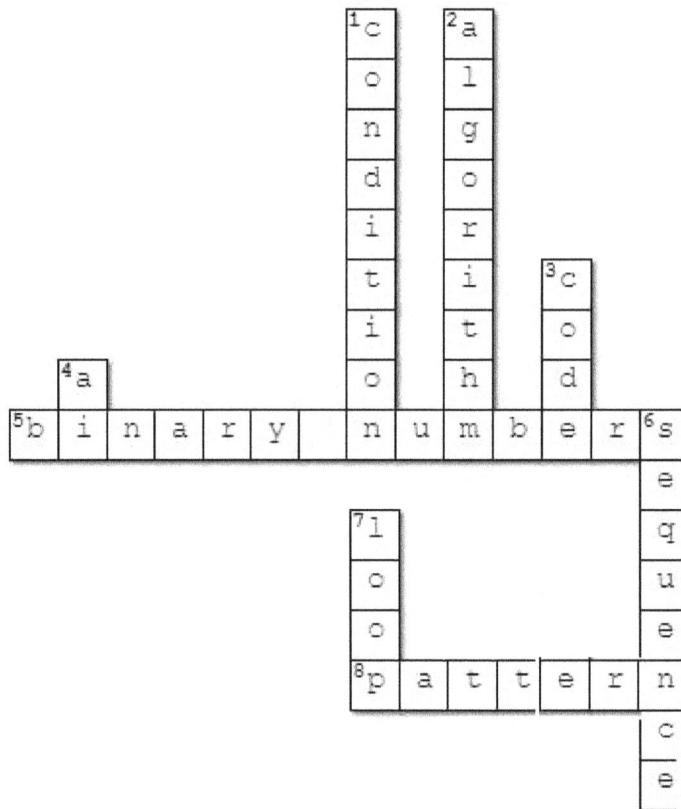

Down:
1. condition
2. algorithm
3. code
6. sequence
7. loop

Across:
5. binary number
8. pattern

Answer Key

Sequence This! <B/>

1. var traffic_light = "red";
2. if(traffic_light == "red")
3. { //comment: Then begin action
4. Print("STOP Moving.");
5. } //comment: Then close action

Crossword Puzzle <B/>

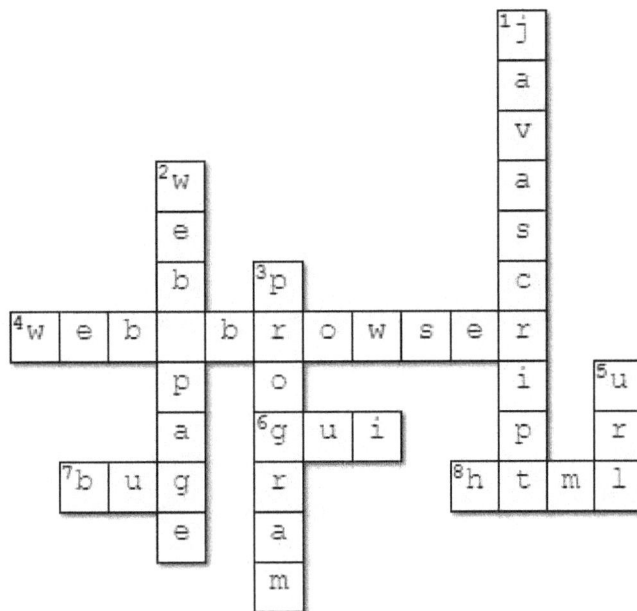

Crossword answers:
- 1 (down): javascript
- 2 (down): webpage
- 3 (down): program
- 4 (across): web browser
- 5 (down): url
- 6 (across): gui
- 7 (across): bug
- 8 (across): html

Decode This! Binary Numbers to Decimal

Binary Value	Decoding Formula								Decimal Values
0 1 1 0	0	+	4	+	2	+	0		6
0 1 1 1	0	+	4	+	2	+	1		7
1 0 0 0	8	+	0	+	0	+	0		8
1 0 0 1	8	+	0	+	0	+	1		9
1 0 1 0	8	+	0	+	2	+	0		10

Answer Key

Star Maze-ing Game - Algorithm Worksheet

One possible solution is…

1. moveForwardOneStep();
2. moveUpOneStep();
3. moveForwardOneStep();
4. moveForwardOneStep();
5. moveForwardOneStep();
6. moveForwardOneStep();
7. moveForwardOneStep();
8. moveDownOneStep();
9. moveForwardOneStep();
10. moveDownOneStep();
11. moveForwardOneStep();

BONUS: Loop Bin
(based on the solution above)

Repeating Pattern 1:
```
Loop( 5 ) //repeat 5 times
{
    moveForwardOneStep();
}
```

Repeating Pattern 2:
```
Loop( 2 ) //repeat 2 times
{
    moveDownOneStep();
    moveForwardOneStep();
}
```

Map The Keywords

1. URL or Web Address | 2. Web Browser | 3. Web Page | 4. GUI | 5. HTML

---

www.ingramcontent.com/pod-product-compliance
Lightning Source LLC
LaVergne TN
LVHW082324080426
835508LV00042B/1539